INSECT SOUP

Bug Poems
by
Barry Louis Polisar

illustrations by David Clark

The Dung Beetle

There's reason for discretion
(So let us be discreet).
No need for explanation;
Just say it likes to eat.

The Tick

It's true the tick
Can make you sick.

When brush is thick,
Leave quick.

Praying Mantis

When sitting down to dine, they say
Many feel the need to pray;
But when you have upon your plate
A meal consisting of your mate
Do you not think it truly coarse
To give thanks to a higher force?

Saddleback Caterpillar

I wonder if *he* thinks it odd
To have a face on both sides of his bod?

Oriental Cockroach

It's different from its cousins.
How so? Ah, now I see.
It loves to eat with chopsticks
And has a yen for tea.

House Fly

Here is the spot where the fly touched down.
She paused too long, that's clear.
Swat went the swatter. Zap! It got her.
Now all that's left is a smear.

Unicorn Beetle

The unicorn beetles
Played in the park,
While Noah was busy
Loading his ark.

Just like the unicorn,
They missed the boat.
But these beetles were lucky;
These beetles could float.

Ants

In my kitchen, by my door
Ants are crawling 'cross my floor.
Along the wall they march in style,
Regimented, single file.

I want them gone but I'm unable
To stop the sacking of my table.
At night I spray and set the traps
But they return for kitchen scraps.

Some are clearly on patrol,
Scaling up the dog food bowl.
They're climbing all around my sink,
Descending downward for a drink.

I see their small antennae rattle,
They've dug in for a long hard battle.
They've even come with queen and throne
And claimed my kitchen as their own.

The Flea

Hiding in the woodland
'Neath brush and under log,
You'll find the flea who frequently
Will hop upon my dog.

Though fleas are very tiny,
They'll wake him every night;
It's not the size that matters
But the fact that they can bite.

Lice

Take my advice
Avoid all lice.

They simply are
Not very nice.

The Roach

Behold the roach; how it survives,
Living life upon the edge;
It hides in cracks and crevices
Beneath the kitchen counter ledge.

It finds a way to live each day;
'Mid poisons, traps and cheap motels,
Then quick takes flight at signs of light
And keeps on guard for human smells.

Le Hotel

Cicada

In all their years
Under the ground,
Deep in the soil
They make no sound.

No wonder when
They come above,
They cry out loud
And search for love.

Though predators
May hear their song,
Their need to sing
Aloud is strong.

To some it's noise
That won't abate,
But it's sweet music
To a mate.

Butterfly

A caterpillar wanted badly
To become a butterfly.
She hated crawling on the ground
And wished that she could flutter by.

She got her wish in time of course.
(A wish she did regret).
She turned into a butterfly,
Then flew into a net.

Millipede

I used to have a millipede;
I kept him for a pet.
I fed him every day at noon
And took him to the vet.

I knitted him a sweater
And made five hundred pair
Of tiny silken slippers
For my millipede to wear.

And though I treated him so well,
He snuck out in the street,
Then muddied up my carpets
When he didn't wipe his feet.

Chiggers

Lie in the ditch
and you may itch,

For out of sight
Lives the mite.

Chiggers repose
Beneath your clothes.

They'll leave a welt
Under your belt,

And while you sleep
They'll burrow deep

And at your seat
Will start to eat.

Poor or rich
You still will itch.

dung beetle—The dung beetle will roll a wad of manure into a ball which it later uses for food. It mates and also lays its eggs in this ball of manure, which provides the larvae with food.

tick—An arachnid, similar to the mite, but larger. Ticks are parasites who attach themselves to animals and suck their blood until they become engorged and fall off. They carry many diseases.

praying mantis—The praying mantis gets its name by the way it holds its forelegs in front of its body in what looks like a position of prayer. The female praying mantis usually attacks and eats the male after they have mated.

saddleback caterpillar—As a defense, the back of the saddleback caterpillar resembles a ferocious looking face.

oriental cockroach—A dark brown roach, thought to have originally come from the Orient.

housefly—Though it does not bite, the housefly is one of the most dangerous and commonest of flies. It feasts on garbage, excrement and filth and transports bacteria and germs on its hairy body and sticky foot pads, spreading disease.

unicorn beetle—The unicorn beetle is a beetle that has a single horn sticking out of his head.

ants—A social insect that lives in colonies that range from a few dozen to hundreds of thousands. Ants have at least one queen, though it is the worker ants that are usually seen.

flea—A wingless leaping insect that bites and sucks the blood of mammals such as dogs, cats and people!

lice—Lice are small, wingless insects such as the body louse, the head louse and the crab louse. Their mouths are particularly adapted for sucking and biting.

cockroach—There are about 1,200 species of cockroaches. They have flat, oval bodies with long antennae and large eyes. They produce an odor by secretions from their glands.

cicada—Often mistakenly called a locust, the cicada nymph buries itself in the ground for as long as seventeen years. It then digs its way out of the ground, sheds its outer shell, and emerges as an adult. Male cicadas produce a song by vibrating the muscles on their abdomens, attracting females.

butterfly—An insect with broad wings which are covered with colorful scales. It generally takes about two to three weeks for the worm-like larva of a caterpillar to turn into a butterfly.

millipede—The millipede does not actually have one thousand legs; at most they have 180 legs and are usually only a few centimeters long.

chiggers—Also known as red bugs, chiggers have six legs and can be found in brushy areas. These mites burrow into people's skin, causing a severe itching sensation when they eliminate their waste.

Insect Soup © 1999 by Barry Louis Polisar
Illustrations © 1999 by David Clark
Published by Rainbow Morning Music
2121 Fairland Road, Silver Spring, Maryland 20904

ISBN # 0-938663-22-4
First Edition

My thanks go to my cousin, Sheldon Biber, as usual, editor extraordinaire; and to my wife, Roni and kids, Evan and Sierra, for all their help, comments and suggestions.